Lamenting the Dream of Lost Love and Lanterns

Poems of love and grief
by

Claire Gathercole

ISBN: 978-0-244-16519-2

PublishNation
www.publishnation.co.uk

*These poems are dedicated to
my late husband, John,
and my ever-loving family*

CONTENTS

A LAMENT

That Loving Feeling – a Lament

And have you lost the feeling
of a hand inside your own –
that sense as fingers move
around to find their comfort
zone and clasp together
to speak of love.

And have you lost that look
that darts from eye to eye
when you know the other
thinks as you do and
knows exactly what it is
that makes you laugh.

And have you lost the sense
of another body nearby yours
when you realise that you
can reach to feel its warmth
and know that touch
will be always welcome.

And have you lost the embrace
of a hug when your whole
body feels enveloped and
set free from care and tension
for one long moment of
release and joyfulness.

And have you lost the words
that murmur soul to soul
and do not need to be
restrained or limited
because there's understanding
there and a loving rare.

LANTERNS

The Lantern

'Giddy with nausea'
    we raced away
        looking for relief
            from the aching, aching.

'Heartbeat and thrill'
    are never enough
        to satisfy our longings
            and relieve the pain.

And pure voices raised
    in song may yet inspire
        but are not the answer
            to our quest.

The darkness caught us
    as we stumbled along
        muddying our way
            but in the distance ...

It was there... a dim
    flicker of light swinging
        in the breeze
            to give us hope.

Lanterns

The choir lanterns are decorated
to diffuse the light
as people browse the building
and long for song to lift
their thoughts above the
mundane dregs of the
mind to heavenly sunlight
shining through stained glass.

The black and white tiles gleam
with polish to encourage
us to explore this place
step by step, discovering
memorials of time past
and folk long forgotten by
the busy bustling world which
hustles without consideration.

The windows of the Chapter House
reflect the trees outside
lush with the green of summer
and secure as they proudly
shade the passersby, whispering
to them of time and events
experienced long ago
and still recalled in quietness.

And voices murmur on outside
as folk explore the cloisters and
stop to greet each other in the
café, reflecting on experiences
from time past and hopes for
years to come if time will
only bend a little and let
the light shine in the darkness.

Holloways

The footfalls beat to the
sound of distant music
and the rustle of clothes
reverberates them through.

The murmurings meditate
and mediate between the
thoughts that wander
through the pilgrimage of minds.

A cough crackles loud
to interrupt the wonderings
and bring them down to the
earthy necessities of life.

And now a louder heavy
insistent foot bears down
while a noisy phone
demands a reply at once.

Holloways cover our heads
and surround our thoughts
with the murmurings
of our farming forbears…

…who struggled through snow
ice and scorching heat
to continue on, so how can
we neglect to do the same.

LOOK

Come... See...

Come... see...
      ...the yellow kingcups in my garden
      pool, which lighten my eyes as I
      realise his tree is in bloom
      again, white and frothy and
      shining in the sun, in time once
      again to welcome his anniversary
      on Shakespeare's Day.

Come... see...
      ...where my solar fountain
      jets up in joyful ecstasy
      with its gentle burble
      rivalling that of the bumble
      bees that already search
      for nectar in the golden
      delicacy of the primroses as
      they face the sun.

Come... see...
      ...where the cherry blossom
      glistens its promise silver
      white upon my golden
      wall to gladden me with
      thoughts of luscious fruit
      if I watch carefully to
      shield its precious kernels
      from that unexpected frost.

The Book Room

You sat in the chair at your desk and watched
the birds, lifting the phone to tell me
they were using the bird bath you gave me,
while the music sang and your pen flowed.

The Book Room we called it and it contained
many shelves of your books, some deep
theological, impenetrable, yellow with age
while others were bursting with new ideas...

My novels and poetry books were housed nearer
the window with the travel and old car books
on the shelves next to your desk with all those
vintage magazines in piles on the floor!

The piano was difficult to house crammed
in beneath the books and scarcely used until
the whole house lit with the joy of children
 and grandchildren sitting together and playing it.

And if the books could talk what would they say?
Did they listen to the phone calls he made
describing detail after detail of a car? Or speaking
to the perplexed hearts of those in trouble?

Is this, was this the hub of the house and if I
change it, as I must, will I lose the essence
of our love, our life together ...?

The Bookcase of my Life

The Honey Bears was the first book
I loved. They were a family and
Mother Bear guarded her babies
fiercely, which I suppose was
important for me to know.

My next favourite was written
on rough war-time paper and
called *Ernest the Elephant.*
He was a trier. He tried to
do many things and I can't
remember whether he succeeded
in the end. It was the endeavour
which was important to me.

So Long - about a wonderful
sausage dog who got stuck was
another favourite and made me
anxious for him, while I laughed
relieved that there was someone
to help him break free.

I had to cheat to get into the
School Library and say I'd read *Alice
In Wonderland.* I hadn't. I had tried
and hated it. It wasn't real. This was
wartime and life was difficult enough
without trying to cope with fantasy.

So teenage adventure books gathered
me up and spat me out. *The Famous Five,*
What Katy Did, and suchlike, until I
discovered romance and magazine 'Love'
stories which made me grow up
and hope ...

... and fear as I read *Tess of the D'Urbevilles*
and realised that there was sorrow deep
in love. Life had to be navigated with care.

I read and underlined so many *Bible* quotes
in red that they still stay with me though
images from *The Pilgrim's Progress* fade
back into the ether of time. How did I
manage to cope with that!

Shakespeare helped me discover
how to laugh at life, as did Mrs Bennett
in *Pride and Prejudice,* though there were
as many tragedies as comedies
and one needed to beware.

The pages of my *Dr Spock* on baby colic
in their first three months were so well
worn by hope for answers that they tore!
Then *The Tiger came to Tea* followed by
The Hobbit and *Lord of the Rings* to keep
up with my children's fantasy escapes.

The *Narnia* books I've read many a time
and frightened too-young children with the
white witch, while finding comfort in
bereavement in *The Last Battle* in these
latter years.

And will *The Waste Land* be the story
of my life? The last twist of the knife?

LEAVES

Leaves may fall

A villanelle for the family

Give me words that sing a song
of air thick with scented bells ..
Leaves may fall but love stays strong

I think back and is that wrong..?
not one good day would I now sell
Give me words that sing that song

And hearts sigh will it be long
while thoughts arise we cannot quell
Leaves may fall but love stays strong

Think of times when we all throng
together and all goes well
Give me words that sing that song

Believe then that we still belong
to each other, for we all gel ..
Leaves may fall but love stays strong

Give me words that sing a song
of times past which went pell mell
and years to come when we will tell
that leaves may fall but love stays strong.

The burnished leaves

His leaves are burning in my sight...
'The autumn is so colourful
this year', my friends delight to say.
The atmospherics must be right
to tinge and burnish every leaf
so that they fill my wondering eyes.

As they arrest my lonely heart
they speak again of joy and warmth
for newly planted we joined hands
and danced to celebrate for him
his fiftieth when all seemed bright -
joyfully joining hands in hope.

It is so painful to remember loving
when the leaves have dropped.

The Corner of the Curtain: a circular psalm

I raise the corner of the curtain   warm and downy with
                                                                    feathers

it covers the calamities   it shields from the icy blast

hiding the sickness and sorrow   protecting from the cruel
                                                                    wind.
---ooo000ooo---

I peer through and watch each little bird   our ever loving
                                                                    friends

flying staunchly with their messages   emailing comforting

seeking deliverance   pleading for help.
---ooo000ooo---

I float on the curtain of their prayers   I feel their soft breath

on this cloud of hope   their fervent desire

as they entreat and entreat again   that I should live

Dusk falls, birds roost   twilight reigns...

      ... until the blackbird sings
                              until the blackbird sings ...

*The red lines and purple lines can either be read straight across or
each colour can be read downwards separately.*

La Marseillaise

(written after the attack in Paris, July 2016)

In my mind I am in their garden –
my dear friends in Auxerre who will be
grieving so much at the terror they
face and puzzled that we are leaving Europe.

In my mind I look for Caroline –
the tortoise searching the undergrowth
near her for a ripe apricot from
their wonderful *délicieux* tree,
le goût of which is surely unique.

In my mind I am walking out with
them to buy some *pain* each fine morning
to eat *pour le petit déjeuner.*
A good habit which I grew to love.

In my mind I think of the ties that
bind us, remembering happy times
when our children played together in
their teens and later visits which still
continue as we all grow older.

But now I find they no longer walk
to buy their daily bread. Last time
I visited they gave me sweet brioche
to break my fast ... and nowadays their
Supermarché sells English cut loaves.

In my mind when La Marseillaise
is played, I sing it too and weep a
tear for their awful predicament.
How can we leave them now and pretend
that we are not part of one another?

The Little Boat

The little boat with its
upturned bow and keel
and merry sail blowing
in the wind brought
joy and hope to those
who watched from the
shore, wondering ...

When it had passed
no trace could be found
nor track of its keel in
the waves and the
watchers could only tell
of the happiness it gave
them, pondering ...

How they wished it
would return and they
became those who
embroidered stories of
the little boat and the
vision of it sailing on
by, dreaming ...

LIGHT

A Pantoum of Eclipses

The last year of the eclipse
we donned those special lenses
so that we could see it well
we sensed the difference they made.

We donned those special lenses
they made us feel a part of it
we sensed the difference they made
we shivered as the sun grew dark.

They made us feel a part of it
we began to understand
we shivered as the sun grew dark
we were totally dependent on its light.

We began to understand
the sun was a capricious god
we were totally dependent on its light
unless we pleaded it would disappear.

The sun was a capricious god
this year's eclipse was partial
I pleaded that it would appear
the shiver of dark sky and bird song ceased.

This year's eclipse was partial
the view on the TV reduced it so
to images of dark sky and strident voice
'The very time of your life' he said.

The view on the TV reduced it so
I held my colander up to the sun
'The very time of your life' he said
The pinpricks of light were crescent shaped.

The image on the paper was my compound loss.

The Bowl

The lines and shapes and colours
burst here and there but it is
the circle of the bowl that draws
the eye and calmly contains
the disparate elements and
makes sense of them.

And do we call them circles or rings?
Rings on the finger speak of love
while bells use their molton circles
to ring out and tell of joy
or sorrow to be learned
and chimed into our lives.

The roundels on the windows
reflect the light and tell a story
that we can appreciate as
the mood takes us and we
spin in and out of life's journey
and solemn thoughts of time's circle.

An Afternoon in the Sun

Beware, beware, the blackbird cries!
The traffic's thoughtless noise
breaks in on me
and is it an aircraft overhead?
The noise is drowning me.

Thank goodness for the tiny bee
still delving petals deep to succour
it. Thank goodness for the
burbling of my pebble pool
which never ceases to whisper   to my heart.

He loved the blackbird's song
but can he hear it now pure
and undefiled by earthbound busyness?
Where is the hush of dawn and dusk
and will the ant still run through   the stillness?

I must get up earlier to meet
my Maker in the quietness and
find the roses which have blossomed
overnight and wonder again at the
perfume in the air and feel
the love in the delights engendered while
I sleep, which bring refreshment   to my soul.

And now the violas spring to life,
lifting their sweet faces to the sun and
waving in the gentle breeze as if expectant
of a smile from me, which they shall have.

How wonderful, the daisies are flowering again
nudged in among the cracks of that ugly
wall and transforming it with their
pink white cheerfulness of   love expressed.

Sunlight and Cream

Stone sifts the sunlight
on the wall ... or does the
wall warm and move the
shadows of the sun

which drift from place to place
with no thought of the
consequence on those
who no longer feel its heat

but are left in sad shade
longing for the warmth
to touch them once again
          light filling their horizon like clotted cream.

Retail Therapy

I was late and my hasty footsteps
echoed in my head as I set out
to search for them among the
crowds thronging the corner
where the clothes were hanging off
the rails and jumbled up.
I'd catch a glimpse first here
then there. They were so quick
exclaiming in delight or annoyance
at this or that. Not my size.
Not my colour. Too big. Too small.
The retail therapy was clicking in...

and then exploding! "Come and
look at this", came a cry. "What do
you think?" "Is it too tight?
Do I look OK in it?" What do you think?"
"Which cubicle are you in?"
"Do come and look, I need advice"

Ah...those were the voices I knew
I found them and joined in!

LIES AND SHADOWS

Shadows

And the photo that she took
of the chasm showed not the
outline of the rocks, but the
ghostly shadows of those
who were present unaware.

She sat in the shadow of her life
and watched it lengthen before her
playing the scenes in her mind
over and over again, looking
for light to illuminate them.

We light the candles one by one
and as they flicker, they stay
our eyes and still our thoughts
as the shadows fade slowly
slowly and we begin to understand.

Walking in the Dark

Light is never really safe.
It illuminates our fears
and makes it quite obvious
that we walk alone.

Darkness can be soft and kind
hiding us from hurtful stabs –
the daylights dripping raw wounds
that can't be hidden.

The star-lit mellow twilight
of dawn and dusk can soon heal
with their secret mysteries
of a Love that cares.

Let the eye begin to see
that the shadows that are feared
can glow to start guiding us
through the harshest day.

Chance

And if we throw the cards
in the air, they might
fall down when the
Big Bang was irrupting
and we could watch.

Or they might fall down
when the Civil War shook
our land and brother
fought with brother
and we would fear.

Or they might fall down
when the Battle of Britain
filled our skies and
the Spitfires saved our
land as we held breath.

Or they might fall down
when we were first in love
and the words spoken or sung
still hang in the air
where we walked that day.

For the past is still there
he told us and if we went
back we could still see
it happening as it did.
It never goes away

And the future too is
there already if we could
but time travel on to
perceive it all –

a mind-boggling view.
So perhaps it is easier
to create a storyline to
fill our imaginations with
a gentler narrative
to explain it all.

Lies

They were my lies at first
        I didn't know they were lies
        as I fought to persuade
        him that he would live.

        It's not what you think,
        I would say. You're not
        like that. It won't happen
        to you.

        Of course I was wrong
        and I must have made
        it worse as he tried
        to agree…

        …and spoke no more of
        his worries or the pain
        and discomfort which
        dodged him.

        Lies cannot live with love.

Echoes

The echo of him reverberates
and then is lost in the balm of
busyness.

The corners of the mind do not
open up the dreams
they simply accumulate
the dust and ashes ...

that will not go away
fogging the future
and hiding the hope we
long to hold in our hands ..

and realise, as the echoes
mock us and silence is
the sadness of that inward
groan which dwells so deep

it cannot be plucked out.

LOSS

Fire and Water at Grenfell Tower

When will the burning stop?
A seemingly endless store of
fire rises and rises to
illuminate our need
and the angry flames of
questions will not be pacified
or quenched by the spurt
of water, which alone can
save us and give us the
means to live.

An infinity of thought can
not be put out however
sweet the water offered
to restore our souls. Nor
can it dowse the sparks
which ignite the indignation
in our hearts that our
protests were not considered
or thought worthy of a
just response.

The people in the tower had
many languages and boundless
stores of knowledge to enrich
us all, with stories which would
have stretched to the shorelines
of the world, and we who are
left are now stunted in our
growth because we did not
nurture them but only gave
them the rules of death.

No Way of Escape

And I see her vulnerable with
age and remember how my mother's
hot tears would lie molten in my heart
and burn fear into my useless legs.
Has she no way of escape either?
Is she locked hard in my nightmare dream?

And once again I grieve as I see her in
my mind's eye wanting to be with us
and join in .. but I could not be the daughter
living nearby that she longed for day by day.
We were each locked in the distance
that separated us and could not break free.

There was no way of escape.

The Fight for Survival

The little boat struggles in the swell
as the wind pulls at our clothing
and the hail batters our hope
of reaching a calm and sunny shore.

Wet and beaten down, all is spoiled
for us as our memory refuses
to relent and there is no birdsong
to relieve our wild imaginings.

Will there be no end to this storm
which enforces us to fight and fight again
for survival as once more relentless
darkness closes in on us...

Don't Hibernate Here

You don't hibernate here
but strive to keep your world
turning, turning day by day
so that you don't disintegrate
and shred those precious
leaves of love which must
live on to feed the generations
that are to come and come again.

When you were young you loved to
make mud pies. It was a sensual
thing. You liked the sticky feel on
your fingers and the relief
when they were washed and
clean again. And now you are
older you still long for that
cathartic feel of things put right.

You have been afraid so many times
and now the world has turned again
and the worst has come. Does that
relieve your fear or do those thoughts
still pinprick you in the night and cause
your heart to shed the tears that dwell
in the well of you where reviving water
can still be found if you will reach for it.

Beneath and Behind

Beneath the tiles of this floor
there are Saxon remains, but also
insects creeping, exploring,
multiplying in ways I cannot
imagine in a world of their
own right down through
rocks and molten lava
to the very core.

Behind me are the memories
of days gone by, waiting
for the shadows of time to
fade and solidify
as I reach back and
handle them with care
waiting for the voice that
calls to sound afresh.

A Fearless Heart

Shall I open up my heart or dwell
in fear? There is no other way to
love but to release and walk with it
even if the night is black.

The fear that stalks our hearts is of love
disappointed or lost or only
discovered when the day has past which
would have brought it to full bloom.

We need the warmth of sunshine in our
soul to illuminate the fear for
what it is – a parasite that means
no good and would then destroy.

Let us show it up and banish it
for fear should be for others not
ourselves and protectionism will not
suffice as love brings joy and pain.

LONGINGS

Twenty-one Today

She holds the balloon for all to see.
This is her special day – a once
in a lifetime occasion and she
wants to make the most of it
and remember the day she was 21.

Her eyes catch mine across the room
and, yes, I remember too my
far-off day when there were no
balloons but flowers galore and
cards and rings and parties.

She is flanked by loving parents
and you can see the pride and
protective care in their eyes.
They want her to remember this
day and their love for her.

Writing the Heart

There is no rest from the longing
that he was still around and
we could sit and laugh together.

I fill my days with a multitude
of friends and we talk and talk
and all seems well until...

...a ray of sun lights the place
where he sat or a blackbird sings
to wake the dawn the way he liked

Your voice is no longer in my head.
I've lost the feel and the smell
of you although I still have clothes
that tell a tale and I can't throw away.

There was the day I woke from
a daytime dream to think you sitting
near and you were not and I was cross
with you and what good's that?

There is no rest from the longing
my brokenness is not the sort that mends.

To My Valentine

I think I prefer you with a smear of grease
or dirt upon your face. It brings your eyes alive.

But I enjoy it too when
you stand up and preach,
lean forward and include
us all, making us think
with you and think again.

I love the way that we can share and share
again our thoughts and fears, our hopes –
and can express them both in words
and touch, our bodies joining to make one whole.

And I still long to be with you,
and to be near
makes the most sense
and is the easiest way
to say
I love you

The Other Room

A year has passed and yet
our life's story still fills my head.
Do grief and sadness ever cease?
My voice droned on giving false hope
as I think back and cannot leave
those times behind me now.

I tried to comfort him
when he lay dying. "I will come
and find you," I said, "as I always
do." The garage was his favourite
place but making bread, taking
phone calls, writing letters …

he was always busy in
the other room … as he is now.

LOVE

We are Dreamers ...

We are dreamers ...
the happy sound of
children's voices echo
laughing in our ears
telling their story.

We are dreamers ..
looking for butterflies
to soar iridescent
with sun on their wings
transforming our world.

We are dreamers ...
harsh boggy ground will
not suck our souls
to blight and destroy
our future hope.

We are dreamers ...
searching for oases
in the desert to
sustain and shelter from
the burning heat.

We are dreamers ...
mountains echo with
love songs which
will not be quieted
but sing in our souls.

Sanctuary

I'm sitting in the quietness
and the fire is burning softly
and I'm waiting and I'm watching
and remembering those I love.

I've been trying to think of giving
and I'm not much good at choosing
but I want them all to know
that I hold them in my love.

I'm preparing and I'm sorting
and I'm emailing and talking
but I want to find the way
to give to those I love.

It's not the presents I would give them
it's not the holly and the ivy
but to help them find that sanctuary
in the presence of His Love.

Love Letters

And what will the love letters tell
when they search them out
and find the words which have
been waiting there these many years ...

to be discovered and dreamt about
again. And what did they mean
those words of love and feelings
long ago treasured and enjoyed ...

and then forgotten. Will the love
live on to re-kindle those that read?

The Party

They arrived before I expected them
but the sun was shining and the
Pimms was ready to be served
and the joy began to flow
as each greeting was enjoyed.

How I had longed to see so
many of them who otherwise
would only have met at my
funeral. No, no, I wanted
to talk and laugh with them.

Families and friends are in
our hopes and fears and we
need to support, love and accept
each other for who we are and
what we want to be.

Our identities are bound up in
one another and are intertwined.
We must hold on to one another
In love and spread that love
abroad to those around.

The world needs love ....

The Dance

We tap the rhythm and take up our chance
It is not hard to do, let's make a stand
We simply fit our footsteps to the dance.

Musicians play and so our lives enhance
With melodies that help us understand
The rhythm we pace to take up our chance.

And we can raise our voices now perchance
With songs and laughter as we clap our hands
And work to fit our footsteps to the dance.

Let's try to make a pattern as we prance
And twirl and whirl and then we jump and land
Pacing the rhythm and taking our chance.

So if our story makes you spare a glance
In our direction, please do join us and
We'll work to fit all footsteps to the dance.

The dance of love is tender, will entrance
And delight us as we make sure we've planned
To pace the rhythm and take up the chance
Which fits in all our footsteps to the dance.

Printed in Great Britain
by Amazon

76468385R00031